D1487493

Microwave Magic
Meals for 1 or 2

Grolier Limited
TORONTO

Contributors to this series:

Recipes and Technical Assistance:
École de cuisine Bachand-Bissonnette
Cooking consultants:
Denis Bissonette
Michèle Émond
Dietician:
Christiane Barbeau
Photos:
Laramée Morel Communications
Audio-Visuelles
Design:
Claudette Taillefer
Assistants:
Julie Deslauriers
Philippe O'Connor
Joan Pothier
Accessories:
Andrée Cournoyer
Writing:
Communications La Griffe Inc.
Text Consultants:
Cap et bc inc.
Advisors:
Roger Aubin
Joseph R. De Varennes
Gaston Lavoie
Kenneth H. Pearson

Assembly:
Carole Garon
Vital Lapalme
Jean-Pierre Larose
Carl Simmons
Gus Soriano
Marc Vallières
Production Managers:
Gilles Chamberland
Ernest Homewood
Production Assistants:
Martine Gingras
Catherine Gordon
Kathy Kishimoto
Peter Thomlison
Art Director:
Bernard Lamy
Editors:
Laurielle Ilacqua
Susan Marshall
Margaret Oliver
Robin Rivers
Lois Rock
Jocelyn Smyth
Donna Thomson
Dolores Williams
Development:
Le Groupe Polygone Éditeurs Inc.

We wish to thank the following firms, PIER I IMPORTS and LE CACHE POT, for their contribution to the illustration of this set.

The series editors have taken every care to ensure that the information given is accurate. However, no cookbook can guarantee the user successful results. The editors cannot accept any responsibility for the results obtained by following the recipes and recommendations given.

No part of this book may be reproduced or transmitted in any form or by any means, electronic or mechanical, including photography, recording, or any information storage or retrieval system, without permission in writing from the publisher.

Canadian Cataloguing in Publication Data

Main entry under title:

Meals for one or two

(Microwave magic ; 22)
Translation of: Repas pour 1 ou 2.
Includes index.
ISBN 0-7172-2443-0

1. Microwave cookery.
I. Series: Microwave magic (Toronto, Ont.) ; 22.

TX832.R4713 1988   641.5'61   C88-094221-5

Copyright © 1988 by Groupe Polygone Éditeurs Inc.
All rights reserved.
Printed and Bound in Canada

Table of Contents

Microwave Magic is a multi-volume set, with each volume devoted to a particular type of cooking. So, if you are looking for a chicken recipe, you simply go to one of the two volumes that deal with poultry. Each volume has its own index, and the final volume contains a general index to the complete set.

Microwave Magic puts over twelve hundred recipes at your fingertips. You will find it as useful as the microwave oven itself. Enjoy!

Note from the Editor

How to Use this Book
The books in this set have been designed to make your job as easy as possible. As a result, most of the recipes are set out in a standard way.

We suggest that you begin by consulting the information chart for the recipe you have chosen. You will find there all the information you need to decide if you are able to make it: preparation time, cost per serving, level of difficulty, number of calories per serving and other relevant details. Thus, if you have only 30 minutes in which to prepare the evening meal, you will quickly be able to tell which recipe is possible and suits your schedule.

The list of ingredients is always clearly separated from the main text. When space allows, the ingredients are shown together in a photograph so that you can make sure you have them all without rereading the list—

another way of saving your **valuable time. In addition, for the more complex recipes we have supplied photographs of the key stages involved either in preparation or serving.**

All the dishes in this book have been cooked in a 700 watt microwave oven. If your oven has a different wattage, consult the conversion chart that appears on the following page for cooking times in different types of oven. We would like to emphasize that the cooking times given in the book are a minimum. If a dish does not seem to be cooked enough, you may return it to the oven for a few more minutes. Also, the cooking time can vary according to your ingredients: their water and fat content, thickness, shape and even where they come from. We have therefore left a blank space on each recipe page in which you can note

the cooking time that suits you best. This will enable you to add a personal touch to the recipes that we suggest and to reproduce your best results every time.

Although we have put all the technical information together at the front of this book, we have inserted a number of boxed entries called **MICROTIPS** throughout to explain particular techniques. They are brief and simple, and will help you obtain successful results in your cooking.

With the very first recipe you try, you will discover just how simple microwave cooking can be and how often it depends on techniques you already use for cooking with a conventional oven. If cooking is a pleasure for you, as it is for us, it will be all the more so with a microwave oven. Now let's get on with the food.

The Editor

Key to the Symbols
For ease of reference, the following symbols have been used on the recipe information charts.

The pencil symbol ✐ is a reminder to write your cooking time in the space provided.

Level of Difficulty

🍴 Easy

🍴🍴 Moderate

🍴🍴🍴 Complex

Cost per Serving

$ Inexpensive

$ $ Moderate

$ $ $ Expensive

Power Levels

All the recipes in this book have been tested in a 700 watt oven. As there are many microwave ovens on the market with different power levels, and as the names of these levels vary from one manufacturer to another, we have decided to give power levels as a percentage. To adapt the power levels given here, consult the chart opposite and the instruction manual for your oven.

Generally speaking, if you have a 500 watt or 600 watt oven you should increase cooking times by about 30% over those given, depending on the actual length of time required. The shorter the original cooking time, the greater the percentage by which it must be lengthened. The 30% figure is only an average. Consult the chart for detailed information on this topic.

Power Levels

HIGH: 100% - 90%	Vegetables (except boiled potatoes and carrots) Soup Sauce Fruits Browning ground beef Browning dish Popcorn
MEDIUM HIGH: 80% - 70%	Rapid defrosting of precooked dishes Muffins Some cakes Hot dogs
MEDIUM: 60% - 50%	Cooking tender meat Cakes Fish Seafood Eggs Reheating Boiled potatoes and carrots
MEDIUM LOW: 40%	Cooking less tender meat Simmering Melting chocolate
DEFROST: 30% **LOW: 30% - 20%**	Defrosting Simmering Cooking less tender meat
WARM: 10%	Keeping food warm Allowing yeast dough to rise

Cooking Time Conversion Chart

700 watts	600 watts*
5 s	11 s
15 s	20 s
30 s	40 s
45 s	1 min
1 min	1 min 20 s
2 min	2 min 40 s
3 min	4 min
4 min	5 min 20 s
5 min	6 min 40 s
6 min	8 min
7 min	9 min 20 s
8 min	10 min 40 s
9 min	12 min
10 min	13 min 30 s
20 min	26 min 40 s
30 min	40 min
40 min	53 min 40 s
50 min	66 min 40 s
1 h	1 h 20 min

* There is very little difference in cooking times between 500 watt ovens and 600 watt ovens.

Cook in Small Quantities— Produce Great Dishes!

Perhaps you are living alone for the first time and the idea of cooking for one is troubling you. Not to worry! Such circumstances, shared by many, can present surprising advantages. Some people appreciate the fact that they can prepare a gourmet meal for themselves without having to consult a household of individuals about the menu. Others feel they can now afford occasional luxury items from the speciality stores—items they could not afford for a larger group.

There are, however, some disadvantages as well. In spite of the growing numbers of people who live alone or with one other person, it is difficult to find cook books designed for cooking in small quantities. Recipes serving four to six people cannot be converted to serve one or two without some careful thought.

Shopping, weekly menu planning and meal preparation are necessary regardless of the number of people involved. What does present a problem is the purchase of perishable food. Many supermarkets offer mainly prepackaged food and it is often difficult to find food packaged in small quantities.

How, then, does one manage to plan meals that are balanced and varied and yet adapted to one's needs? This problem is exactly what this volume is all about: cooking for one or two! We hope it will provide you with some good ideas and sound advice.

It is important to establish at the outset a list of the food needed for the week's menus, thus preventing last-minute scrambling for needed items. A shopping list is an important tool in the efficient planning of meals. The shopping guide on page 12 was compiled to assist you and contains useful information about which products to buy and what characteristics to look for.

This volume also provides several charts to guide you in terms of portion sizes, food storage and cooking times. Various preparation techniques are presented to help you in your culinary efforts as well.

Cooking with a microwave oven is especially suited to people who have little time to spend in the kitchen. Once you have mastered certain rules applicable to conversion of quantities, you will be able to adapt most recipes and produce a banquet for one or an intimate dinner for two. If you live alone, why not invite a few friends to share that leg of lamb you bought on sale from the butcher? A gourmet meal, a Sunday brunch or an everyday dinner—you'll be equal to anything.

Don't be afraid to add color to your kitchen and dining room—make them pleasant places to spend your time preparing meals and then enjoying them by livening them up with flowers, plants and colorful accessories. Even the most ordinary dish will look festive served on attractive china!

To all you gourmet cooks out there: good luck!

Conversion: A Simple Operation

If the word "conversion" is synonymous, in your mind, with complicated mathematical equations, you can relax! Converting a meal for four into a meal for two requires only a bit of judgment and some simple arithmetic.

Have you ever had to give up on a dish because the quantities and the cost exceeded your requirements and your budget? How many delectable recipes have never reached the table when all that was needed was a simple conversion? We hope this book will offer you some practical tricks to help you adapt your recipes.

Cooking in small quantities has some advantages. It allows one to consider extravagant recipes that would be difficult to make for a large group without ruining the weekly budget; when you cook for one or two, small luxuries are affordable.

Although understandable, concern about buying large cuts of meat or whole large vegetables is unnecessary when one considers modern storage and preserving methods. Let's consider freezing, for example: as long as you follow some basic rules, you can freeze a leg of lamb for several months. Large vegetables such as cauliflower and broccoli can be cut up into pieces of equal size and frozen. Leftovers can be frozen and used for future meals. In this way, you can take advantage of the sales offered by the supermarkets each week. Also, freezing will preserve seasonal foods; you will thus be able to have a varied diet during the winter months, using fresh vegetables frozen in August and treating yourself to strawberries picked in the summer.

Most recipes offered in cook books can be doubled or halved. To halve a recipe, it is obvious that the quantity given for each ingredient is divided by two. But there are some ingredients that do not follow this rule—eggs, for example. It is difficult to divide 3 eggs into 2 equal parts; you would therefore use 2 eggs. As well, our method of measuring ingredients sometimes makes it difficult to be precise in reducing the original amount to half. See the conversion chart below for guidelines to measuring quantities so that they are as close to half as possible.

Converting Quantities to Half

Original Quantity	Half Quantity
15 mL (1 tablespoon)	7 mL (1-1/2 teaspoons)
50 mL (1/4 cup)	30 mL (2 tablespoons)
75 mL (1/3 cup)	37 mL (2 tablespoons + 1-1/2 teaspoons)
175 mL (3/4 cup)	90 mL (6 tablespoons)

From Four to Two

Although the quantities of most ingredients in recipes are reduced in proportion to the number to be served, the same is not necessarily true of the preparation, cooking and standing times. How these are affected varies from one dish to another. There are many factors to consider when cooking with the microwave: thickness, density, weight, sugar and fat content, amount of liquid added, positioning of food during cooking and so on. It is therefore impossible to establish one single rule for reducing recipes in all microwave cooking. See the reduced recipe below and the accompanying chart for an example of conversions in terms of preparation, cooking and standing times.

Note that power levels always remain the same and standing times may or may not change.

Recipe For Chicken With Parsley

	For 4 people	For 2 people
Preparation Time	30 min	20 min
Number of Servings	4	2
Cooking Time	28 min	16 min
Standing Time	5 min	5 min
Power Level	100%, 70%	100%, 70%

Ingredients	For 4 people	For 2 people
Chicken, cut into pieces	1 chicken, 1.3 kg (3 lb)	1 chicken breast, halved
oil	30 mL (2 tablespoons)	30 mL (2 tablespoons)
onions, sliced	250 mL (1 cup)	125 mL (1/2 cup)
mushrooms, sliced	250 mL (1 cup)	125 mL (1/2 cup)
carrots, grated	125 mL (1/2 cup)	50 mL (1/4 cup)
celery, diced	2 stalks	1 stalk
garlic cloves, crushed	1	1 small
white wine	250 mL (1 cup)	125 mL (1/2 cup)
parsley, chopped	30 mL (2 tablespoons)	15 mL (1 tablespoon)
thyme	2 mL (1/2 teaspoon)	1 mL (1/4 teaspoon)
bay leaf	1	1 small

Your Shopping Guide

Once the weekly menu is established, a trip to the supermarket is the next step in meal planning. The choice of ingredients and the decisions as to required quantities demand careful attention. For this reason, we are providing you with a shopping guide to the foods, both fresh and processed, that you will need.

Try to choose a supermarket where you can buy food in bulk, therefore, in whatever amounts you require. If this is impossible, don't hesitate to ask for smaller portions of meat, vegetables or cheese than those already packaged when you are shopping. A courteous manager will be only too happy to accommodate you. But enough chatter—let's go shopping!

Vegetables

To begin with, let's have a look at the vegetables. Often, people living alone refuse to buy a head of cauliflower or a package of fresh spinach for fear of wasting a large portion. Although understandable, such fears are groundless because it is possible to freeze most vegetables. However, it is important to freeze them as quickly as possible to preserve their flavor and nutrients. Most fresh vegetables should be blanched before freezing (see page 15). Fresh vegetables are, of course, to be preferred, but with a freezer you can take advantage of the weekly sales offered by the supermarkets. If you buy frozen vegetables, buy them in bags rather than in cartons; it is much easier to remove small quantities from a bag without defrosting the entire package. Make sure you reseal the bag so that it is airtight, to prevent freezer burn.

Meat

Meat that is fresh and of top quality is always the best choice. The various cuts of beef, pork, veal and lamb allow for a great variety in your daily menus. Like vegetables, large cuts of meat can be cut into individual portions and frozen. But you will be able to buy the most tender cuts to use fresh because the cost for small quantities will not be prohibitive.

Beef

Many different cuts of beef are available. However, the cut is not the only factor one should consider; the age of the animal, the fat content, the firmness and the color of the meat are also important. If in doubt, ask your butcher for advice as to quality when buying beef—a sensible precaution since you naturally want only the best.

Pork

Pork is not divided into as many categories as beef. In this country, pork is usually a product of young animals and is, for the most part, very tender. You can recognize good quality pork by its pink color and firm texture. The loin has a somewhat lighter color while the cuts from the shoulder and butt are generally a deeper pink.

Veal

As with pork, veal is also a product of animals slaughtered at a young age. However, this is not an absolute guarantee of tenderness. Check the color of the meat to determine the age of the animal. Young veal is not marbled and is uniformly pale pink in color. Veal that has a redder tinge and is more marbled comes from an older animal and will be less tender.

Lamb

Make sure you choose lamb that is deep pink in color and firm in texture. You will be able to recognize lamb that is not fresh by its soft texture. When chops or stew are not on the menu, a leg of lamb will serve your purposes very well, especially as you can use it to prepare different dishes.

Poultry

Poultry is generally economical. It includes a variety of birds of different sizes and flavors and can be prepared in an infinite number of ways—offering a great opportunity for variety in your menus. Certain wild birds such as quail and duck that are now being bred offer a range of interesting flavors. The legs and breast are ideal portions for one or two people. And don't forget that a whole bird can be cut into serving pieces and stored in the freezer for several weeks (see the chart on page 14).

Seafood

Do you like seafood but don't alway know what you want when you get to the fish market? Perhaps these few hints will help you in your choices. Whatever you choose, make sure it is fresh. If you buy a whole fish for the freezer, you must scale it before freezing. Fish fillets are recommended as they are the easiest cuts to divide into one or two portions.

Canned Goods

Canned vegetables, meats and fish can spoil if they are not used within a short time after opening. To prevent waste, buy small cans. And always keep some in reserve; they can be useful for last-minute meal preparation.

Storing Food

Any procedure carried out in the kitchen demands certain precautions. Freezing, for instance, must be done according to specific rules if one wants to preserve the food's flavor and texture.

Containers used for freezing should not be much larger than the food they will contain; too much air in the container causes ice crystals to form in the food, which promotes deterioration. Make sure you label the containers, identifying the contents, the date of freezing and the maximum storage time; this information will help you use your frozen foods while they are at their best.

Using freezer bags with a vacuum-sealing machine is, of course, the most efficient method of packaging. However, such equipment is not always available; still, you can get good results by forcing as much air as possible from the bags manually and sealing them tightly. Round containers (tube pans, casserole dishes, etc.) allow for a better distribution of microwaves so defrosting will be more rapid and more even. An extra bonus is that you won't have to transfer the food from

Storage Times for Pork

Cut	Refrigerator	Freezer
Rib end	2 to 3 days	2 to 3 months
Chops	2 to 3 days	3 to 4 months
Ham	5 to 7 days	2 months
Ground pork	2 to 3 days	2 to 3 months
Sausages	4 to 5 days	
Bacon	7 days	Not recommended

Storage Times for Poultry

Fresh Poultry	Refrigerator	Freezer
Boneless chicken	1 to 2 days	6 to 7 months
Chicken pieces	1 to 2 days	4 to 5 months
Boneless turkey	1 to 2 days	4 to 5 months
Turkey pieces	1 to 2 days	2 to 3 months*
Whole guinea fowl	1 to 2 days	3 months**
Whole quail	1 to 2 days	3 months**

* Fresh poultry that has been cut into serving pieces should be washed after defrosting.

** Vacuum-packed.

these containers to other dishes for cooking.

Cooked dishes such as macaroni and cheese, stews and so on can be placed in freezer bags and then put into suitable casserole dishes. All you need do is close the bag, expel the air, seal and place in the freezer. As mentioned earlier, you should not use containers that are

any larger than necessary. Portions for one or two people should therefore be frozen in small containers.

Consult the above charts for recommended storage times for different cuts of pork and poultry in both the refrigerator and freezer. See page 16 for charts giving the same information for veal, beef and fish.

How to Package Meat for Freezing

For good results when freezing meat, use vacuum sealing equipment to eliminate any air or moisture. If such equipment is not available, remove as much air as possible by drawing it out with a straw and seal with ties that do not contain any metal strips.

For easy separation of steaks, patties or fillets of meat or fish place a sheet of waxed paper between each piece. Stack them in bunches of 2 to 4 and wrap the stack in aluminum foil.

Cooked dishes and ground beef can be frozen in small round containers. If the container has no cover, place the food in a freezer bag in the container, remove the air from the bag and seal tightly.

How to Prepare Vegetables for Freezing

Most vegetables should be blanched before freezing. Blanching stops the action of the enzymes in vegetables that cause deterioration and discoloration.

To blanch vegetables, place them in an appropriate container and add the required amount of water. Cook in the microwave oven for half the time required to cook them completely, stirring once halfway through the blanching time. Place the blanched vegetables in ice cold water immediately to stop the cooking. Drain and freeze in tightly sealed bags.

Consult the chart opposite for recommendations as to container sizes, water quantities and appropriate times for blanching some specific vegetables.

**Blanching of Vegetables
(Power Level: 100%)**

Vegetable	Quantity	Container Size	Water Quantity	Time (min)
Asparagus	450 g (1 lb)	2 Liters	50 mL (1/4 cup)	1 1/2 to 2
Beans	450 g (1 lb)	1.5 Liters	75 mL (1/3 cup)	4 1/2 to 6
Broccoli*	450 g (1 lb)	1.5 Liters	30 mL (2 tablespoons)	2 to 3
Cauliflower*	450 g (1 lb)	2 Liters	30 mL (2 tablespoons)	2 to 3
Spinach (washed)	450 g (1 lb)	2 Liters	no water	1 1/2 to 2

* Broccoli and cauliflower should be cut into 2.5 cm (1 in) flowerets.

Storage Times for Veal, Beef and Fish

Storage Times for Veal

Cut	Refrigerator	Freezer
Cooked veal	7 days	3 months
Cubes	2 days	3 to 4 months
Escallops	24 hours	3 months
Ground veal	2 days	3 to 4 months
Loin and rib chops	2 days	3 to 4 months
Offal	1 to 2 days	3 months
Pork chops, etc.	3 days	6 to 8 months
Roasts	3 days	8 to 9 months
Side ribs	2 days	3 to 4 months

Storage Times for Beef

Cut	Refrigerator	Freezer
Cooked beef	7 days	3 months
Ground beef	2 days	3 to 6 months
Offal	1 to 2 days	3 months
Roasts	3 days	8 to 12 months
Steak	3 days	6 to 9 months
Stewing beef	2 days	6 months

Storage Times for Fish

Type of fish	Freezer
Fat: herring, mackerel, perch, salmon, smelt, sturgeon, trout, tuna	3 months
Medium fat: halibut, Norway haddock, turbot	4 months
Lean: cod, goby, haddock, pickerel, plaice, whiting	6 months

Defrosting Food

After taking the time to prepare your menus and to carefully prepare your food for freezing, you certainly don't want to waste your efforts by improper defrosting methods. Often this is exactly what happens. Unfortunately, some people feel, wrongly, that defrosting requires no special precautions—an attitude we would like to change.

Improper defrosting can alter the quality of food, and even spoil it entirely. Now, let's see how we can avoid such an unhappy experience.

When you are defrosting food that will produce a lot of juice, it is important to remove it from its packaging. Meat, poultry and fish all belong to this category. To avoid having meat sitting in its own juices and thus defrosting unevenly, place it on a bacon rack or an inverted saucer in a larger dish.

The weight of the food to be defrosted must also be considered. Since defrosting times depend on weight, it is important to know the weight of each package to be defrosted. The defrosting chart on pages 18 and 19 will help you to determine defrosting times for different foods, according to weight. It is important to note that you must divide the total defrosting time into 2 or 3 periods in the microwave with periods of standing time equal to a quarter of the total defrosting time in between.

The way you arrange the food to be defrosted is very important as well. For even defrosting, try to arrange food in a circle. Microwaves are more concentrated around the edges of a dish and any food in the center thaws more slowly. If you are defrosting items that are not uniform in shape, such as chops, the thickest parts should be placed toward the outside of the dish. The thinner parts are then toward the center, where the microwaves are less intense.

Please note that the final standing time is an important part of the entire defrosting process.

MICROTIPS

For Perfect Defrosting
Defrosting in the microwave oven is a very speedy process. However, to ensure even defrosting of meat, a power level of no more than 30% is recommended. Meat should be completely thawed before cooking.

  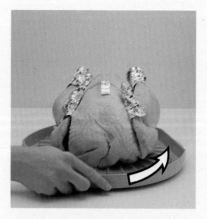

To prevent parts of the meat from sitting it its juices and defrosting faster than the rest, place the meat on a rack or bacon rack which, because of its grooved surface, allows the juices to drain away. If a rack is not available, an inverted saucer in a larger dish will serve the purpose.

Before defrosting, protect the less fleshy parts of the bird (the ends of the legs, wing tips and along the breast bone) and of roasts (the ends and bony areas) with strips of aluminum foil. Similarly, protect the extremities of a whole fish during defrosting.

Halfway through the defrosting cycle, give the dish a half-turn in order to ensure the equal distribution of the microwaves and therefore the even defrosting of the food.

Defrosting Guide for Different Foods

Food	Power Level	Defrosting Time
Beef		
Steaks	30%	6 to 8 min/450 g (1 lb); 4 to 6 min/225 g (1/2 lb)
Cubes	30%	5 to 10 min/450 g (1 lb); 4 to 8 min/225 g (1/2 lb)
Ground beef	30%	5 to 10 min/450 g (1 lb); 3 to 4 min/225 g (1/2 lb)
Pork		
Chops	30%	3 to 6 min/450 g (1 lb); 2 to 4 min/225 g (1/2 lb)
Spare ribs	30%	3 to 6 min/450 g (1 lb); 2 to 4 min/225 g (1/2 lb)
Ham (slices)	30%	3 to 6 min/450 g (1 lb); 2 to 4 min/225 g (1/2 lb)
Ground pork	30%	3 to 6 min/450 g (1 lb); 2 to 4 min/225 g (1/2 lb)
Veal		
Chops and cutlets	30%	3 to 6 min/450 g (1 lb); 2 to 4 min/225 g (1/2 lb)
Cubes	30%	4 to 6 min/450 g (1 lb); 3 to 4 min/225 g (1/2 lb)
Escallops	30%	3 to 6 min/450 g (1 lb); 2 to 4 min/225 g (1/2 lb)
Ground veal	30%	3 to 6 min/450 g (1 lb); 2 to 4 min/225 g (1/2 lb)

Defrosting Guide for Different Foods

Food	Power Level	Defrosting Time
Lamb		
Chops and cutlets	30%	4 to 6 min/450 g (1 lb); 3 to 5 min/225 g (1/2 lb)
Cubes	30%	4 to 6 min/450 g (1 lb); 3 to 5 min/225 g (1/2 lb)
Ground lamb	30%	3 to 6 min/450 g (1 lb); 2 to 4 min/225 g (1/2 lb)
Poultry		
Chicken legs (2 legs, 100 g each)	30%	5 to 7 min
Chicken breasts (2 breast, 225 g each)	30%	7 to 9 min
Fish		
Whole fish (medium)	30%	5 to 8 min/450 g (1 lb); 3 to 4 min/225 g (1/2 lb)
(small)	30%	3 to 5 min/450 g (1 lb); 2 to 3 min/225 g (1/2 lb)
Pieces of fish	30%	4 to 7 min/450 g (1 lb); 3 to 4 min/225 g (1/2 lb)
Fillets (separated)	30%	5 to 8 min/450 g (1 lb); 3 to 4 min/225 g (1/2 lb)
Pasta		
Cooked pasta, without sauce (1 portion)	70%	3 min
(2 portions)	70%	5 min
Cooked pasta, with sauce (1 portion)	70%	4 min
(2 portions)	70%	6 min
Cooked rice		
125 mL (1/2 cup)	70%	2 to 3 min
250 mL (1 cup)	70%	4 to 8 min

Note: The defrosting time should be divided into 2 or 3 periods in the microwave with periods of standing time equal to a quarter of the total defrosting time in between.

Cooking a Small Feast

To make sure each meal is a feast in itself, you must follow certain rules when cooking in your microwave oven. While this volume deals with cooking for one or two, we must emphasize that you don't necessarily divide cooking times by two when cutting a recipe in half. Make sure you know the exact time of cooking required in each recipe.

As with larger quantities, the cut, density, and amount must be considered when calculating cooking times for smaller portions. Foods that are more dense cook more slowly. It is obviously preferable to cook foods of similar density and shape together to obtain a uniform result. Because microwaves are more concentrated at the outer edges of a dish than in the center, the food at the edges cooks more quickly than that in the middle. It is then important to place the thicker or denser parts of any food toward the outside edge of the dish.

Vegetables

As well as offering a very rapid method of cooking, the microwave oven preserves the nutrients in vegetables. Since it is unnecessary to cook them in large amounts of liquid, vegetables that have a high water content (zucchini, spinach, etc.) retain all their water-soluble vitamins. With this method of cooking, vegetables retain their color and flavor, and remain crisp. Vegetables should always be cooked covered so that they don't lose any moisture. The cooking chart on page 105 will give you the cooking times required for various vegetables.

Meats

As in traditional cooking, microwave cooking depends on the cut of meat as well as the weight. As well, the fat and water content will determine cooking times as both fat and water attract microwaves. Meat that is very fat will cook more quickly than lean meat; the same thing applies to meat that produces a lot of juice or that contains a large amount of sugar—ham, for instance—because sugar also attracts the microwaves. The internal temperature of the meat prior to cooking as well as the amount of bone it contains will also affect the cooking time.

Poultry

As with meat, poultry is best cooked on a rack in a dish where the cooking juices can collect. You can get a lovely golden color by using a browning dish to sear chicken pieces before cooking them in the oven. Color can also be obtained by brushing poultry with such other agents as barbecue sauce, browning agents for gravies, paprika or butter before cooking. Whole birds and those cut into serving pieces should be placed so that they will cook evenly. It is also a good idea to cover the less meaty parts with strips of aluminum foil.

Fish

Fish has a very delicate flesh and does not require much time to cook; too much cooking will dry it out. You must check it at regular intervals during cooking. The fish is done when it can be flaked esily with a fork.

Meats should be raised in their cooking dish. To cook large roasts, such as the leg of lamb shown here, use a rack or bacon rack to allow the juices to drain away. This prevents parts of the meat from sitting in the juices and cooking prematurely. If a rack is unavailable, an inverted saucer in the cooking dish will serve the same purpose.

To ensure the even cooking of a leg of lamb, protect the thinner parts with strips of aluminum foil, covering a surface of 5 cm (2 inches) at either end. Place the fatty side of the leg on the bottom of the dish for the first period of cooking.

For even cooking of any meat, flip it over and give the dish a half-turn midway through the cooking time.

Pork Pâté

Level of Difficulty	🍴🍽
Preparation Time	5 min*
Cost per Serving	**$**
Number of Servings	2
Nutritional Value	402 calories 21.5 g protein 25.7 g lipids
Food Exchanges	3 oz meat 3 fat exchanges
Cooking Time	10 min
Standing Time	none
Power Level	100%
Write Your Cooking Time Here	

*The pork pâté should be refrigerated before serving.

Ingredients
125 mL (1/2 cup) soft bread crumbs
125 mL (1/2 cup) milk
225 g (8 oz) ground pork
1 onion, grated
1 mL (1/4 teaspoon) cloves
1 mL (1/4 teaspoon) ginger
1 clove garlic, crushed
salt and pepper to taste

Method
— In a bowl, combine the breadcrumbs and milk; mix well.
— Add all the other ingredients.
— Cook for 8 to 10 minutes at 100%; stirring every 4 minutes.
— Blend well with a fork; for a smoother consistency use an electric mixer.
— Put into a mold and chill before serving.

Salmon Mousse

Level of Difficulty	🍴🍴 🍴🍴
Preparation Time	15 min*
Cost per Serving	$
Number of Servings	2
Nutritional Value	345 calories 32 g protein 23.2 g lipids
Food Exchanges	4 oz meat 4 fat exchanges
Cooking Time	2 min
Standing Time	none
Power Level	100%
Write Your Cooking Time Here	

* The salmon mousse should be refrigerated for 3 to 4 hours before serving.

Ingredients
1 213 mL (7 1/2 oz) can salmon
10 mL (2 teaspoons) gelatin
125 mL (1/2 cup) water
125 mL (1/2 cup) 18% cream
2 egg yolks
5 mL (1 teaspoon) lemon juice
salt and pepper to taste
2 egg whites

Method
— Sprinkle gelatin over the surface of the water and set aside to soften for 5 minutes; stir.
— Heat for 1 minute at 100% and stir to dissolve the gelatin; set aside.
— Heat the cream for 1 minute at 100%; beat with a whisk while adding the egg yolks, gelatin and lemon juice.
— Flake the salmon and mash it into a purée; add to the above mixture and season.
— Beat the egg whites until they form stiff peaks and fold them gently into the salmon mixture.
— Chill a mold in cold water and then add the salmon mixture.
— Refrigerate for 3 to 4 hours before serving.

The salmon mousse is very easy to prepare and calls for ordinary ingredients that you will have in your pantry. To save time and steps, gather all the ingredients before starting to prepare the recipe.

Flake the salmon, mash it into a purée and add to the mixture of egg yolks and cream.

Gently fold the beaten egg whites into the salmon mixture.

27

Garlic Bread

Level of Difficulty	🍴
Preparation Time	15 min
Cost per Serving	$
Number of Servings	2
Nutritional Value	502 calories 38 g carbohydrates 34 g lipids
Food Exchanges	2 1/2 bread exchanges 7 fat exchanges
Cooking Time	6 min
Standing Time	17 min
Power Level	100%
Write Your Cooking Time Here	

Ingredients
1 small loaf Italian bread
3 cloves garlic, crushed
90 mL (6 tablespoons) butter
15 mL (1 tablespoon)
Parmesan cheese, grated
5 mL (1 teaspoon) Italian spices
2 mL (1/2 teaspoon) paprika
15 mL (1 tablespoon) parsley, chopped

Method
— Place the butter and garlic in a dish; cook at 100% for 1-1/2 to 2 minutes, stirring once during cooking.
— Add the Parmesan cheese, spices, paprika and parsley; mix well.
— Allow to stand for 15 minutes.
— Cut the loaf diagonally, without cutting through the bottom crust.
— Spread the slices with the butter mixture and cook for 3 to 4 minutes at 100%.
— Let stand for 2 minutes.

Cut the loaf in diagonal slices without cutting through the bottom crust so that the loaf will keep its shape.

MICROTIPS

Some Tips on Freezing
In order to avoid overcooking, pasta and rice should be undercooked before freezing. Reheating will finish the cooking process and the food will retain a firm and agreeable consistency. Cooked dishes that call for garnishes of breadcrumbs or grated cheese are better frozen without them; the garnishes can be added just before placing them in the oven. Foods that tend to dry out, such as chicken, can be brushed with a fine coating of oil so that they will retain their texture, even after long periods in the freezer. Sauces that need to be thickened should be thickened with flour rather than cornstarch; cornstarch can deteriorate in a sauce when left in a freezer for too long.

Tomato Soufflé

Level of Difficulty	
Preparation Time	20 min
Cost per Serving	$
Number of Servings	2
Nutritional Value	211 calories 12.6 g protein 13.1 g carbohydrate
Food Exchanges	2 oz meat 1 vegetable exchange 1 fat exchange
Cooking Time	4 min
Standing Time	1 min
Power Level	100%, 50%
Write Your Cooking Time Here	

Ingredients
2 large tomatoes
2 small eggs
10 mL (2 teaspoons) butter
10 mL (2 teaspoons) flour
75 mL (1/3 cup) milk
30 mL (2 tablespoons)
cottage cheese
15 mL (1 tablespoon)
Parmesan cheese, grated
5 mL (1 teaspoon) parsley,
chopped
pinch thyme
salt and pepper to taste
Sauce:
5 mL (1 teaspoon) wine
vinegar
15 mL (1 tablespoon)
ketchup
pinch basil

Method
— Scoop the pulp out of the tomatoes; set the shells and pulp aside.
— Separate the yolks and whites of the eggs and set aside.
— Melt the butter for 30 seconds at 100%; add the flour and mix well.
— Beating with a whisk, add the milk.
— Cook for 45 to 60 seconds at 100%, stirring once during the cooking time.
— Add the cottage cheese, Parmesan cheese, parsley and thyme; mix well.
— Blend in the egg yolks,

season and set aside.
— Beat the egg whites until they form stiff peaks.
— Mix the ingredients for the sauce.
— Add 5 mL (1 teaspoon) of the sauce to the beaten egg whites; set the remaining sauce aside.
— Add the egg whites to the cheese mixture and fold in gently; spoon it into the tomato shells.
— Place the stuffed tomatoes in a dish and cook at 50% for 2 to 3

minutes, giving the dish a half-turn halfway through the cooking time.
— Let stand for 1 minute.
— Put the tomato pulp through a sieve and add it to the remaining sauce.
— Serve the tomatoes with the sauce.

For good results with this delicate recipe, assemble all the ingredients before beginning.

Stuff the tomato shells with the cheese and egg white mixture and cook.

31

Beef with Orange

Level of Difficulty	
Preparation Time	15 min
Cost per Serving	**$**
Number of Servings	2
Nutritional Value	350 calories 30.9 g protein 17 g lipids
Food Exchanges	3 oz meat 1/2 vegetable exchange 1/2 fruit exchange 3 fat exchanges
Cooking Time	27 min
Standing Time	3 min
Power Level	100%, 50%, 70%
Write Your Cooking Time Here	

Ingredients
salt and pepper to taste
22 mL (1 1/2 tablespoons) flour
225 g (8 oz) beef, cut into cubes 1.5 cm (1/2 in) thick
30 mL (2 tablespoons) butter
1 small onion, finely chopped
1/2 green pepper, finely chopped
150 mL (2/3 cup) beef broth
zest, juice and pulp of 1 orange

Method
— Add salt and pepper to the flour; shake the cubes of meat in the seasoned flour.
— Preheat a browning dish for 7 minutes at 100% and melt the butter for 30 seconds at 100%.
— Sear the meat cubes; add the onion and green pepper.
— Cover and cook at 50% for 5 or 7 minutes, stirring once during the cooking time.
— Add the broth, zest, juice and pulp of the orange; stir vigorously.
— Cover and cook at 70% for 15 to 20 minutes or until the meat is tender, stirring twice during cooking.
— Let stand for 3 minutes and serve.

This easy-to-prepare recipe calls for ingredients that you are likely to have on hand.

Flour the cubes of meat before searing in a browning dish with melted butter.

After searing the meat, add the onion and green pepper.

Bologna and Beef Rolls

Level of Difficulty	🍴
Preparation Time	15 min
Cost per Serving	**$**
Number of Servings	2
Nutritional Value	399 calories 22.6 g protein 22 g carbohydrates
Food Exchanges	3 oz meat 2 vegetable exchanges 1/2 bread exchange 2 1/2 fat exchanges
Cooking Time	9 min
Standing Time	3 min
Power Level	100%, 70%
Write Your Cooking Time Here	

Ingredients
115 g (4 oz) ground beef
4 slices of bologna
30 mL (2 tablespoons) onion, finely chopped
30 mL (2 tablespoons) celery, finely chopped
30 mL (2 tablespoons) instant rice
30 mL (2 tablespoons) chili sauce
15 mL (1 tablespoon) dried parsley
250 mL (1 cup) tomato soup, undiluted
salt and pepper to taste

Method
— In a bowl, mix the beef, onion, celery, rice and chili sauce.
— Place a quarter of the mixture on each bologna slice.
— Roll the bologna slices up and secure with toothpicks.
— Place the rolls in a dish and set aside.
— Add the parsley to the tomato soup and season.
— Cook at 100% for 3 minutes, stirring once during the cooking time.
— Pour the sauce over the bologna rolls.
— Cover and cook for 4 to 6 minutes at 70%. After 3 minutes of cooking time, rearrange the rolls so that those in the center are toward the outside of the dish and continue to cook.
— Let stand for 3 minutes.

This inexpensive recipe can be prepared in a jiffy. Here are the ingredients you will need to assemble before starting it.

Roll each bologna slice up and secure it with a toothpick.

MICROTIPS

Reheating Individual Portions
Reheating individual portions in a microwave is much quicker than reheating a dish containing several servings. Allow 1 minute reheating time for an individual portion at room temperature and 2 minutes for one straight from the refrigerator.

Beef Bourguignon

Level of Difficulty	
Preparation Time	20 min
Cost per Serving	$ $
Number of Servings	2
Nutritional Value	445 calories 27.7 g protein
Food Exchanges	3 oz meat 1/2 vegetable exchange 4 fat exchanges
Cooking Time	38 min
Standing Time	5 min
Power Level	100%, 50%
Write Your Cooking Time Here	

Ingredients
225 g (8 oz) beef, cut into cubes
30 mL (2 tablespoons) flour
30 mL (2 tablespoons) butter
15 mL (1 tablespoon) oil
50 mL (1/4 cup) leeks, white parts only, sliced
50 mL (1/4 cup) pearl onions
50 mL (1/4 cup) carrots, finely sliced
1 clove garlic, crushed
250 mL (1 cup) red wine
pinch marjoram
15 mL (1 tablespoon) parsley, chopped
salt and pepper to taste
15 mL (1 tablespoon) cognac

Method
— Flour the cubes of meat.
— Preheat a browning dish for 7 minutes at 100%; add the butter and heat for 30 seconds at 100%.
— Sear the meat cubes in the butter; remove, place them in a casserole and set aside.
— Heat the browning dish for 4 minutes at 100% and add the oil.
— Sear the vegetables and garlic.
— Cover and cook at 100% for 4 minutes, stirring once during the cooking time.
— Add the wine, marjoram and parsley; season to taste.
— Cook for 3 minutes at 100%.
— Heat the cognac for 20 seconds at 100%, light with a match and pour over the meat cubes to flambé.
— Add the vegetable mixture and reduce the power to 50%.
— Cook at 50% for 20 to 30 minutes, stirring once during the cooking time.
— Let stand for 5 minutes and serve.

Ground Beef Casserole

Level of Difficulty	🍴
Preparation Time	20 min
Cost per Serving	$
Number of Servings	2
Nutritional Value	414 calories 25 g protein 14.3 g carbohydrate
Food Exchanges	3 oz meat 2 vegetable exchanges 3 fat exchanges
Cooking Time	18 min
Standing Time	2 min
Power Level	100%
Write Your Cooking Time Here	

Ingredients
225 g (8 oz) ground beef
30 mL (2 tablespoons) butter
50 mL (1/4 cup) onions, sliced
50 mL (1/4 cup) potatoes, cut in cubes
50 mL (1/4 cup) carrots, cut in cubes
50 mL (1/4 cup) rutabaga, cut in cubes
150 mL (2/3 cup) tomato sauce
pinch marjoram
pinch basil
pinch oregano
salt and pepper to taste

Method
— Place the butter in a dish and add all the vegetables.
— Cover and cook for 4 to 6 minutes at 100%; stir once during the cooking time and set aside.
— In another dish, cook the ground beef for 4 to 5 minutes at 100%; break up the meat with a fork once during the cooking time and again at the end.
— Add the beef to the vegetables as well as all other ingredients and mix well.
— Cook at 100% for 5 to 7 minutes, stirring once during the cooking time.
— Let stand for 2 minutes before serving.

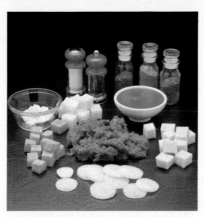

This simple recipe can be prepared in less than 25 minutes. Here are the necessary ingredients.

Cook the onions, potatoes, carrots and rutabaga with butter in a covered dish.

Use a fork to break up the ground beef once during the cooking time and again at the end.

Chicken with Cumin

Level of Difficulty	🍴🍴
Preparation Time	10 min
Cost per Serving	$
Number of Servings	2
Nutritional Value	386 calories 31.6 g protein 2.4 mg iron
Food Exchanges	3 oz meat 1/2 vegetable exchange 4 fat exchanges
Cooking Time	18 min
Standing Time	3 min
Power Level	100%, 70%
Write Your Cooking Time Here	

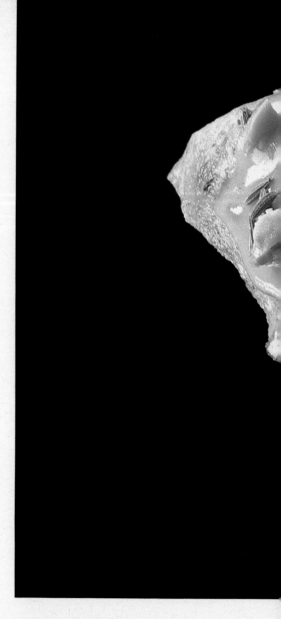

Ingredients
1 whole chicken breast, boned, skinned and cut in half
45 mL (3 tablespoons) butter
1 small onion, sliced
15 mL (1 tablespoon) flour
125 mL (1/2 cup) chicken broth
2 mL (1/2 teaspoon) cumin
10 mL (2 teaspoons) peanut butter
15 mL (1 tablespoon) peanuts
pepper to taste

Method
— Preheat a browning dish for 7 minutes at 100%; add the butter and heat for 30 seconds at 100%.
— Sear the chicken breasts; remove and set aside.
— Add the onions to the browning dish, cover and cook for 2 minutes at 100%.
— Sprinkle the flour over the onion and mix well.
— Add the chicken broth and mix again.
— Cook for 2 minutes at 100%; stir once during the cooking time.
— Add the cumin and peanut butter; season to taste and whisk.
— Put the chicken breasts back into the dish with the sauce; cover and reduce the power to 70%.
— Cook at 70% for 8 to 12 minutes, giving the dish a half-turn midway through the cooking period.
— Sprinkle the peanuts over the mixture and cover again.
— Allow to stand for 3 minutes before serving.

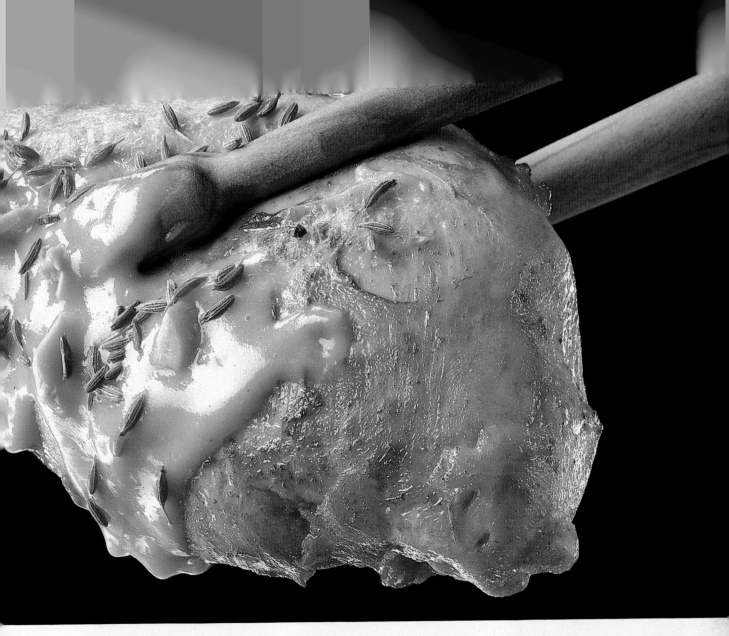

A combination of these ingredients produces a highly original dish in less than 30 minutes.

After cooking the onions for 2 minutes at 100%, sprinkle with flour and mix well.

Return the chicken breasts to the dish with the sauce and proceed to the next step.

Oriental Chicken

Level of Difficulty	
Preparation Time	20 min
Cost per Serving	$
Number of Servings	2
Nutritional Value	444 calories 29.5 g protein
Food Exchanges	3 oz meat 2 vegetable exchanges 4 fat exchanges
Cooking Time	7 min
Standing Time	3 min
Power Level	100%
Write Your Cooking Time Here	

Ingredients
225 g (8 oz) white meat of chicken, cut in strips
50 mL (1/4 cup) oil
1/2 green pepper, cut in strips
1/2 red pepper, cut in strips
1 small onion, sliced
2 mL (1/2 teaspoon) ginger, finely chopped
1/2 clove garlic, finely chopped
75 mL (1/3 cup) chicken broth
15 mL (1 tablespoon) cornstarch
30 mL (2 tablespoons) cold water
4 mushrooms, sliced

Method
— Preheat a browning dish for 7 minutes at 100%; add the oil and heat for 30 seconds at 100%.
— Sear the chicken, peppers and onion; add the ginger and garlic and stir.
— Add the broth, cover and cook at 100% for 3 to 5 minutes, stirring once during the cooking time.
— Dissolve the cornstarch in the cold water and add to the mixture.
— Cook at 100% for 2 minutes, stirring once during the cooking.
— Add the mushrooms and stir.
— Cover and let stand for 3 minutes.

To save time and steps, gather all the necessary ingredients before starting this recipe.

Sear the chicken, peppers and onion in the oil in a browning dish and continue to cook as directed.

Add the mushrooms, then cover and allow 3 minutes' standing time to complete the cooking.

Chicken Paupiettes

Level of Difficulty	
Preparation Time	15 min
Cost per Serving	$
Number of Servings	2
Nutritional Value	398 calories 33.3 g protein 2.4 mg iron
Food Exchanges	3 oz meat 1 vegetable exchange 1 bread exchange 1 1/2 fat exchanges
Cooking Time	13 min
Standing Time	none
Power Level	100%, 90%
Write Your Cooking Time Here	

Ingredients
1 whole chicken breast, boned, skinned and cut in half
15 mL (1 tablespoon) butter
30 mL (2 tablespoons) green pepper, chopped
30 mL (2 tablespoons) red pepper, chopped
30 mL (2 tablespoons) mushrooms, chopped
30 mL (2 tablespoons) celery, chopped
1/2 clove garlic, crushed
125 mL (1/2 cup) fine breadcrumbs
salt and pepper to taste
paprika

Béchamel Sauce
10 mL (2 teaspoons) butter
10 mL (2 teaspoons) flour
125 mL (1/2 cup) milk
salt and pepper to taste

Method
— Prepare the béchamel sauce first by melting the butter in a dish for 30 seconds at 100%.
— Add the flour and mix well.
— Add the milk and beat with a whisk; season to taste.
— Cook the sauce at 100% for 1 to 2 minutes, whisking twice during the cooking time; set aside.
— To prepare the stuffing, place the butter in a dish

and add the vegetables and garlic; cover and cook at 100% for 2 to 3 minutes, stirring once during the cooking time.
— Add the breadcrumbs and season; mix well and set aside.
— Place the chicken breasts between sheets of waxed paper and pound them until quite thin.
— Place equal amounts of the vegetable mixture on each piece of chicken; roll up and secure with toothpicks.
— Sprinkle the rolls with paprika and place on a rack in a suitable dish.
— Cover and cook for 2 minutes at 90%.
— Give the dish a half-turn and cook for 2 to 4 minutes longer.
— Reheat the béchamel sauce for 1 minute at 100%, stirring once during the cooking time.
— Serve the rolled chicken breasts covered with béchamel sauce.

Without doubt, this exceptional recipe will be a great success. Gather all these ingredients together before starting.

Stuffed Cornish Game Hen

Level of Difficulty	🍴
Preparation Time	20 min
Cost per Serving	$
Number of Servings	2
Nutritional Value	440 calories 40.7 g protein ines 3.1 mg iron
Food Exchanges	6 oz meat
Cooking Time	25 min
Standing Time	5 min
Power Level	70%
Write Your Cooking Time Here	

Ingredients

1 Cornish game hen, 900 g (2 lb)
50 mL (1/4 cup) soft breadcrumbs
50 mL (1/4 cup) milk
50 mL (1/4 cup) sausage meat, cooked
1 small onion, finely chopped
1 clove garlic, crushed
1 small egg, beaten
paprika

Method

— Soak the breadcrumbs in the milk and add the sausage meat, onion, garlic and egg; mix well.
— Stuff the hen with above mixture and truss it; sprinkle with paprika.
— Place the hen on a rack, breast side down.
— Cook uncovered for 10 minutes at 70%.
— Turn the hen over, breast side up.
— Continue to cook for 10 to 15 minutes at 70%.
— Allow the hen to stand for 5 minutes before serving.

⇒

Stuffed Cornish Game Hen

Gather all these ingredients to obtain a very refined dish in less than an hour.

Mix the ingredients for the stuffing: breadcrumbs, milk, sausage meat, onion, garlic and egg.

Stuff the Cornish hen with the mixture.

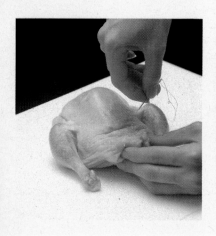

Truss the bird so that it will keep its shape during cooking.

Place the hen on a rack, breast side down.

Turn the hen over, breast side up, before the second stage of cooking.

MICROTIPS

Defrosting Chicken Pieces
To defrost chicken pieces, begin by removing any twist ties containing metal and place the package in the oven. Remove the wrapping as soon as possible. Halfway through, drain and give the chicken a half-turn. Continue to defrost for one quarter of the remaining time. Separate the pieces and continue the cycle, making sure that the thicker parts are toward the outside of the dish. Allow 5 minutes' standing time and wash the chicken pieces with cold water before cooking. Don't forget to divide the defrosting time into several equal periods interspersed with standing times equivalent to one quarter of the total defrosting time.

Chicken Rolls Stuffed with Crab

Ingredients

1 whole chicken breast, cut in half
115 g (4 oz) crab meat
2 green onions, sliced
15 mL (1 tablespoon) parsley, chopped
1 large egg, beaten
50 mL (1/4 cup) breadcrumbs

Level of Difficulty	🍴🍴
Preparation Time	20 min
Cost per Serving	$ $
Number of Servings	2
Nutritional Value	285 calories 41.8 g protein 2.2 mg iron
Food Exchanges	3.5 oz meat 1/4 bread exchange
Cooking Time	10 min
Standing Time	2 min
Power Level	70%
Write Your Cooking Time Here	

Method

— Remove the bones and skin from the chicken breasts.
— Place the chicken breasts between sheets of waxed paper and pound until thin, being careful not to tear them.
— In a bowl, mix the crab meat, green onions, parsley and half the beaten egg.
— Spread a thin layer of the stuffing on each chicken breast.
— Roll tightly and secure with a toothpick.
— Dip each roll into the remaining beaten egg, then roll in the breadcrumbs.
— Place the chicken rolls on a rack and cook for 4 minutes at 70%.
— Give the dish a half-turn and continue cooking at 70% for 4 to 6 minutes.
— Let stand for 2 minutes.

53

Spareribs with Sweet and Sour Sauce

Level of Difficulty	🍴
Preparation Time	10 min
Cost per Serving	$
Number of Servings	2
Nutritional Value	383 calories 9.1 g protein 4.4 mg iron
Food Exchanges	2 oz meat 1 vegetable exchange 3 fruit exchanges
Cooking Time	37 min
Standing Time	5 min
Power Level	70%, 50%
Write Your Cooking Time Here	

Ingredients
900 g (2 lb) spareribs, cut in small pieces
125 mL (1/2 cup) water
1 onion, finely chopped
2 cloves garlic, finely chopped
50 mL (1/4 cup) ketchup
50 mL (1/4 cup) brown sugar
50 mL (1/4 cup) molasses
50 mL (1/4 cup) lemon juice
5 mL (1 teaspoon) dry mustard

Method
— Place the ribs in a dish and add the water.
— Cover and cook at 70% for 14 to 17 minutes, stirring once during the cooking time.
— While the ribs are cooking, mix all the other ingredients in a bowl to make the sauce.
— Remove the ribs from the oven and drain.
— Pour the sauce over the ribs and stir.
— Cook for 15 to 20 minutes at 50%, stir twice during cooking.
— Allow to stand for 5 minutes.

Here are all the necessary ingredients to produce a dish that will, without doubt, add an exotic touch to your menu.

First cook the spareribs in water for 14 to 17 minutes at 70%.

Pour the sweet and sour sauce over the drained spareribs.

Stir the ribs twice during the last stage of cooking to make sure they are evenly cooked.

Pork Chops with Prunes

Level of Difficulty	
Preparation Time	15 min*
Cost per Serving	$
Number of Servings	2
Nutritional Value	582 calories 29.8 g protein 2.2 mg iron
Food Exchanges	3 oz meat 1 1/2 fruit exchanges 6 fat exchanges
Cooking Time	24 min
Standing Time	none
Power Level	100%, 50%
Write Your Cooking Time Here	

Ingredients
2 pork chops, butterflied
6 prunes
5 mL (1 teaspoon) lemon juice
cold water
30 mL (2 tablespoons) flour
salt and pepper to taste
50 mL (1/4 cup) butter
50 mL (1/4 cup) cider
15 mL (1 tablespoon) red currant jelly
50 mL (1/4 cup) 18% cream
15 mL (1 tablespoon) parsley, chopped

* The prunes should be soaked for 8 to 10 hours before cooking.

58

Method
— Place the prunes and
lemon juice in a bowl;
add enough cold water to
cover and allow to soak
for 8 to 10 hours.
— After soaking, heat the
prunes for 8 to 10
minutes at 100% or until
boiling. Stir twice during
the cooking. Set aside.
— Mix the flour, salt and
pepper; set aside.
— Preheat a browning dish
for 7 minutes at 100%;
add the butter and heat
for 30 seconds at 100%.
— Sear the chops, remove
from the dish and set
aside.
— Sprinkle the flour mixture
into the browning dish
and stir.

— Add the cider and beat
with a whisk; cook for 1
minute at 100%.
— Add the chops, cover and
reduce the power to
50%.
— Cook for 10 to 12
minutes, turning the
chops over halfway
through the cooking time.
— Remove the chops and
keep them warm.
— Add the red currant jelly
and cream to the cooking
juices; stir and cook for 1
minute at 100%.
— Add the parsley; if the
sauce is too thick, add a
bit of the prune liquid.
— Serve the chops with the
sauce and drained prunes.

MICROTIPS

Cooking Frozen Foods
Whatever recipe you
prepare, it is important
to remember that frozen
foods take longer to
cook than those that are
defrosted. You must
also remember that
times indicated in the
recipes in this volume
are for foods that are
not frozen. If you are
using frozen foods, you
will have to adjust your
cooking times
accordingly.

Pork Chops with Prunes

This recipe for pork chops will soon become one of your specialties. Here are all the ingredients required for its preparation.

After soaking the prunes for 8 to 10 hours in lemon juice and water, bring them to a boil.

Turn the pork chops over halfway through the cooking time to make sure they cook evenly.

MICROTIPS

The Temperature Probe
Some microwave ovens are equipped with a probe that automatically monitors the internal temperature of meat. Before placing in the oven, insert the probe into the center of the meat. Make sure the probe is not touching fat or bone as this would give a false reading. Set the probe at the desired internal temperature; once this is reached the oven switches off automatically.

To obtain an exact reading and therefore the desired degree of doneness, insert the probe into the center of the meat. Don't forget that after the standing time, the internal heat will have distributed itself and the reading on the probe may indicate a higher temperature.

If you do not have a temperature probe, the next best tool is a meat thermometer that can be used in microwave ovens. (Never leave a thermometer with any metal on it in the oven.) Remove the meat from the oven after it is partially cooked and insert the microwave-safe thermometer. Continue cooking until the thermometer indicates the desired temperature. Remove the meat from the oven, cover with aluminum foil, shiny side in, and let it stand for approximately 10 minutes.

Ham Glazed with Orange

Ingredients
1 ham slice, center cut, 2.5 cm (1 in) thick
15 mL (1 tablespoon) honey
10 mL (2 teaspoons) orange zest
10 mL (2 teaspoons) orange juice

Level of Difficulty	🍴
Preparation Time	5 min
Cost per Serving	$
Number of Servings	2
Nutritional Value	243 calories 18.5 g protein 0.7 mg iron
Food Exchanges	3 oz meat 1/2 fruit exchange
Cooking Time	12 min
Standing Time	2 min
Power Level	50%
Write Your Cooking Time Here	✏️🍎

Method
— With a fork, pierce the ham slice in several places and place in a baking dish.
— Combine the honey, orange zest and juice, mix well and pour over the ham.
— Cover and cook at 50% for 8 to 12 minutes or until cooked to your liking. Turn the slice over after 5 minutes of cooking.
— Let stand for 2 minutes and serve.

Pork Tenderloin Oriental Style

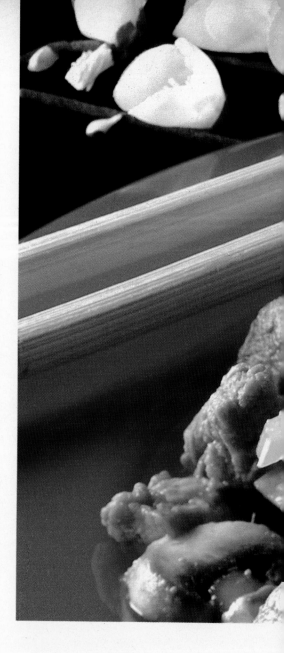

Level of Difficulty	🍴
Preparation Time	20 min*
Cost per Serving	$
Number of Servings	2
Nutritional Value	253 calories 23 g protein 2.7 mg iron
Food Exchanges	3 oz meat 1 vegetable exchange
Cooking Time	10 min
Standing Time	5 min
Power Level	70%, 100%
Write Your Cooking Time Here	

*The meat should be left to marinate for 1 hour at room temperature or 8 hours in the refrigerator before cooking.

Ingredients
225 g (8 oz) pork tenderloin
125 mL (1/2 cup) chicken broth
1 stalk celery, sliced diagonally
salt and pepper to taste
115 g (4 oz) mushrooms, sliced
Marinade:
10 mL (2 teaspoons) cornstarch
15 mL (1 tablespoon) soy sauce
10 mL (2 teaspoons) wine vinegar
5 mL (1 teaspoon) honey
5 mL (1 teaspoon) fresh ginger, sliced
1 clove garlic, crushed

Method
— Cut the pork tenderloin into strips.
— In a bowl, mix all ingredients for the marinade.
— Marinate the pork for 1 hour at room temperature or 8 hours in the refrigerator in a covered bowl; stir occasionally.
— Remove the meat and set the marinade aside.
— Place the pork in a dish, add half the chicken broth and the celery; cover and cook at 70% for 6 to 8 minutes, stirring once during the cooking time.
— Strain the marinade and add the remaining chicken broth; mix and add to the meat.
— Cook at 100% for 1 to 2 minutes or until the sauce thickens, stirring twice, and season.
— Add the mushrooms, cover and allow to stand for 5 minutes.

This recipe is simplicity itself. Gather all the required ingredients before beginning.

Marinate the meat for 1 hour at room temperature or 8 hours in the refrigerator in a covered bowl; stir occasionally.

At the end of the cooking time add the mushrooms; cover and allow to stand for 5 minutes before serving.

63

Pork Chops with Fine Herbs

Level of Difficulty	🍴🍴
Preparation Time	10 min
Cost per Serving	$
Number of Servings	2
Nutritional Value	334 calories 41.6 g protein 1.5 mg iron
Food Exchanges	4.5 oz meat
Cooking Time	12 min
Standing Time	2 min
Power Level	70%
Write Your Cooking Time Here	

Ingredients
4 pork chops, 90 g (3 oz) each
15 mL (1 tablespoon) fine herbs
pepper to taste
50 mL (1/4 cup) breadcrumbs

Method
— Add the fine herbs and pepper to the breadcrumbs and mix well.
— Coat the chops with the crumb mixture and place on a bacon rack, making sure that the thicker part of each chop is toward the outside edge.
— Cook for 8 to 12 minutes at 70%; turn the chops over and give the dish a half-turn after 5 minutes of cooking time.
— Let stand for 2 minutes and serve.

Quick and easy to prepare, this recipe requires only a few ingredients.

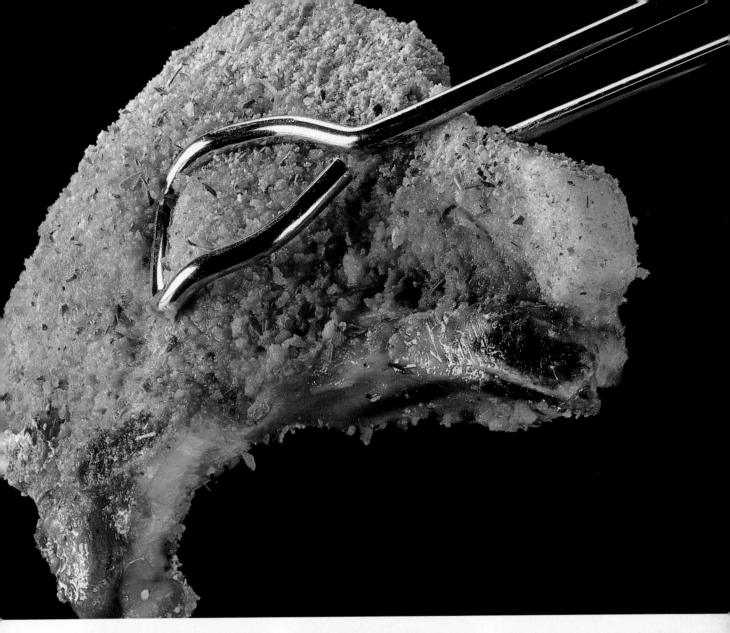

Coat the chops with the mixture of pepper, herbs and breadcrumbs.

Place the chops on a bacon rack so that the thicker parts are placed toward the outside edge.

Turn the chops over after 5 minutes to ensure even cooking.

Haddock Fillets with Mushroom Sauce

Level of Difficulty	🍴
Preparation Time	10 min
Cost per Serving	$
Number of Servings	2
Nutritional Value	344 calories 19.7 g protein 2.6 g lipids
Food Exchanges	2.5 oz meat 1/2 vegetable exchange 3 fat exchanges
Cooking Time	8 min
Standing Time	2 min
Power Level	90%, 100%
Write Your Cooking Time Here	🍎✏️

Ingredients
225 g (8 oz) haddock fillets
30 mL (2 tablespoons) butter
125 mL (1/2 cup)
mushrooms, sliced
10 mL (2 teaspoons) flour
1 mL (1/4 teaspoon) paprika
125 mL (1/2 cup) 18% cream
15 mL (1 tablespoon) parsley,
chopped
salt and pepper to taste

Method
— Place the fillets in a dish,
  making sure the thicker
  parts are toward the
  outside edge.
— Cover and cook at 90%
  for 3 to 4 minutes, giving
  the dish a half-turn
  midway through the
  cooking time.
— Allow to stand for 2
  minutes.
— Place the butter in
  another dish and add the
  mushrooms; cook for 2
  minutes at 100%.
— Sprinkle the flour and
  paprika over the
  mushrooms and mix.
— Add the cream to the
  mixture and stir.
— Cook at 100% for 2
  minutes, stirring once
  during the cooking time.
— Sprinkle with parsley and
  season to taste.
— Serve the haddock fillets
  with the sauce.

Combine these ingredients to produce a well-balanced, nutritious meal in less than 20 minutes.

Place the fish fillets in a dish, making sure the thicker parts are toward the outside edge.

Cook the mushrooms and sprinkle with flour and paprika before adding the cream.

Halibut Steaks

Level of Difficulty	🍴
Preparation Time	5 min*
Cost per Serving	$
Number of Servings	2
Nutritional Value	337 calories 37.5 g protein 0.8 mg iron
Food Exchanges	5 oz meat
Cooking Time	7 min
Standing Time	1 min
Power Level	70%
Write Your Cooking Time Here	

* Fish should be left to marinate for 3 hours in the refrigerator before cooking.

Ingredients
2 halibut steaks, 225 g (8 oz) each
30 mL (2 tablespoons) white wine
15 mL (1 tablespoon) lemon juice
15 mL (1 tablespoon) oil
salt and pepper to taste

Method
— In a bowl, mix the white wine, lemon juice, oil, salt and pepper.
— Place the steaks in this mixture and allow to marinate, covered, for 3 hours in the refrigerator, turning the steaks over twice.
— Remove the steaks from the marinade and set aside.
— Place the steaks on a bacon rack, making sure the thicker parts are toward the outside edge. Brush with half the marinade.
— Cook, uncovered, for 3 minutes at 70%.
— Turn the steaks over and brush with the remaining marinade.
— Continue to cook for 3 to 4 minutes at 70% or until the steaks are just cooked.
— Allow to stand for 1 minute before serving.

White wine, lemon juice, oil, salt and pepper are the only ingredients required to give an incomparable flavor to halibut steaks.

Cover and allow the steaks to marinate in the mixture for 3 hours in the refrigerator, turning them over twice.

Place the steaks on a bacon rack, making sure that the thicker parts are toward the outside edge.

When the steaks are turned over, halfway through the cooking time, brush them with the remaining marinade.

Sole Fillets Stuffed with Shrimp

Level of Difficulty	🍴🍴 🍴🍴
Preparation Time	15 min
Cost per Serving	$ $
Number of Servings	2
Nutritional Value	209 calories 29.5 g protein 1.9 mg iron
Food Exchanges	3.5 oz meat
Cooking Time	6 min
Standing Time	2 min
Power Level	70%
Write Your Cooking Time Here	

Ingredients
2 sole fillets, 225 g (8 oz) each
115 g (4 oz) shrimp, cooked and chopped
30 mL (2 tablespoons) breadcrumbs
15 mL (1 tablespoon) butter, melted
10 mL (2 teaspoons) parsley, chopped
5 mL (1 teaspoon) lemon juice
salt and pepper to taste
paprika

Method
— In a bowl mix the shrimp, breadcrumbs, butter, parsley and lemon juice; season to taste.
— Spread half the mixture over each sole fillet.
— Roll the fillets up and secure with toothpicks.
— Place the rolled fillets on a rack in a baking dish and sprinkle with paprika.
— Cook at 70% for 4 to 6 minutes, giving the dish a half-turn halfway through the cooking time.
— Let stand for 2 minutes and serve.

The combination of these ingredients complements the delicate texture as well as the flavor of sole.

Mix the shrimp, breadcrumbs,
butter, parsley, lemon juice
and seasoning to make a
stuffing for the fillets of sole.

Roll the fillets up and secure
with toothpicks.

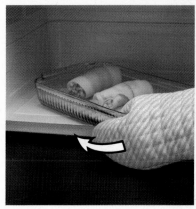

Give the baking dish a half-
turn halfway through the
cooking time to ensure even
cooking.

Fillet of Sole Creole Style

Level of Difficulty	🍴
Preparation Time	15 min
Cost per Serving	**$**
Number of Servings	2
Nutritional Value	149 calories 17.7 g protein 0.7 mg iron
Food Exchanges	2.5 oz meat 1 vegetable exchange
Cooking Time	11 min
Standing Time	3 min
Power Level	100%
Write Your Cooking Time Here	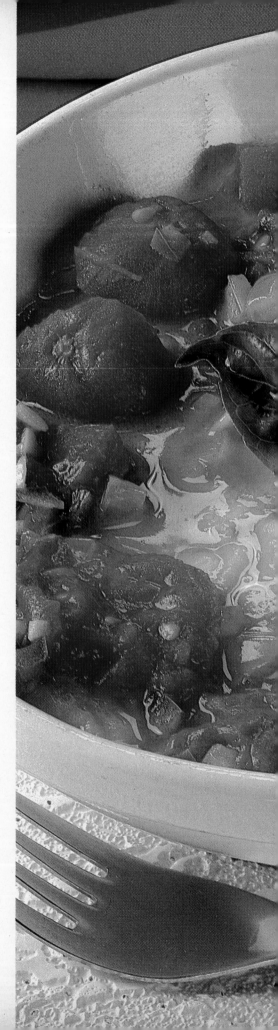

Ingredients

225 g (8 oz) sole fillets
15 mL (1 tablespoon) butter
30 mL (2 tablespoons) onion, chopped
30 mL (2 tablespoons) celery, chopped
30 mL (2 tablespoons) green pepper, chopped
1 clove garlic, chopped
125 mL (1/2 cup) tomatoes, peeled and coarsely chopped
pepper to taste

Method

— Place the butter in a dish; add the onion, celery, green pepper and garlic.
— Cover and cook at 100% for 2 minutes, stirring once during the cooking time.
— Add the tomatoes; cover and continue cooking at 100% for 3 minutes, stirring once during cooking.
— Remove half of this mixture and place the fillets in the dish.
— Cover the fillets with the remaining half of the mixture; add pepper to taste.
— Cover and cook for 4 to 6 minutes at 100%, giving the dish a half-turn midway through the cooking.
— Allow to stand for 3 minutes and serve.

74

Lamb Chops English Style

Level of Difficulty	
Preparation Time	10 min
Cost per Serving	$ $
Number of Servings	2
Nutritional Value	538 calories 32.1 g protein 2.2 mg iron
Food Exchanges	4 oz meat 1 vegetable exchange 5 fat exchanges
Cooking Time	14 min
Standing Time	none
Power Level	100%, 70%
Write Your Cooking Time Here	

Ingredients
4 lamb chops
50 mL (1/4 cup) butter
1 small onion, chopped
30 mL (2 tablespoons) flour
125 mL (1/2 cup) chicken broth
5 mL (1 teaspoon) red currant jelly
5 mL (1 teaspoon) mint sauce
30 mL (2 tablespoons) 35% cream
salt and pepper to taste

Method
— Preheat a browning dish for 7 minutes at 100% and add the butter; heat for 30 seconds at 100%.
— Sear the chops; cover and cook at 70% for 6 to 8 minutes, giving the dish a half-turn halfway through the cooking time.
— Remove the chops and set aside.
— Add the onion to the butter in the browning dish; cover and cook for 2 minutes at 100%.
— Sprinkle the onion with flour and stir to mix well.
— Add the chicken broth and stir again; cook at 100% for 2 minutes, stirring once during the cooking.
— Add the red currant jelly, mint sauce and cream; mix well and season to taste.
— Put the chops back in the browning dish; cover and heat through for 1 to 2 minutes at 100%.

With these few ingredients you can produce a great tasting lamb dish in less than 30 minutes.

MICROTIPS

Microwaves and Liquids
There are several factors that determine the effect of microwaves on food. Besides thickness, density, weight, sugar and fat content, the amount of liquid is a very important factor. In effect, the water content in the food as well as the amount of liquid to be added in a recipe will have a direct bearing on the power level, cooking time and cooking method. Generally speaking, when food has a high water content and when a lot of liquid is called for in the recipe, the microwave action will be slower and cooking times will be longer.

Veal with Vegetables

Level of Difficulty	🍴
Preparation Time	20 min
Cost per Serving	$ $
Number of Servings	2
Nutritional Value	715 calories 50.5 g protein 7.6 mg iron
Food Exchanges	6 oz meat 3 vegetable exchanges 4 fat exchanges
Cooking Time	10 min
Standing Time	3 min
Power Level	100%
Write Your Cooking Time Here	

Ingredients
250 mL (1 cup) veal, cut into strips
15 mL (1 tablespoon) butter
1 green pepper, cut into strips
1 onion, sliced
1 clove garlic, chopped
250 mL (1 cup) mushrooms, sliced
175 mL (3/4 cup) tomato sauce
1 mL (1/4 teaspoon) oregano
pinch basil
salt and pepper to taste
30 mL (2 tablespoons) oil

Method
— Put the butter in a dish; add the green pepper, onion and garlic.
— Cover and cook for 2 minutes at 100%.
— Add the mushrooms and continue to cook at 100% for 2 minutes, stirring once during the cooking. Set aside.
— Combine the tomato sauce, oregano, basil, salt and pepper, and mix well. Set aside.
— Preheat a browning dish for 7 minutes at 100%; add the oil and sear the veal strips.
— Add the vegetables and tomato sauce to the meat.
— Cover and cook at 100% for 4 to 6 minutes, stirring once during cooking.
— Let stand for 3 minutes.

This recipe for veal with vegetables calls for ordinary ingredients, ones that you are likely to have on hand. To save time and unnecessary effort, assemble them before beginning to prepare the recipe.

Add the mushrooms to the partially cooked green pepper, onion and garlic mixture. Cook and set aside.

Sear the strips of veal in a preheated browning dish in oil before adding the vegetables and tomato sauce to finish off the cooking.

Lamb Meat Loaf

Level of Difficulty	🍴
Preparation Time	20 min
Cost per Serving	$
Number of Servings	2
Nutritional Value	250 calories 29 g protein 2.8 mg iron
Food Exchanges	3 oz meat 1/2 fat exchange
Cooking Time	8 min
Standing Time	3 min
Power Level	100%, 70%
Write Your Cooking Time Here	

Ingredients
225 g (8 oz) ground lamb
50 mL (1/4 cup) rice, cooked
30 mL (2 tablespoons) tomato juice
1 small egg, beaten
1/2 clove garlic, crushed
30 mL (2 tablespoons) onion, finely chopped
15 mL (1 tablespoon) chili sauce
2 slices bacon, cut in half

Method
— Combine all the ingredients except the bacon and mix well.
— Put equal amounts of the meat mixture into 2 ramekins of the same size and press down with the palm of your hand.
— Place the bacon slices on top of the meat.
— Put the ramekins in the oven and cook for 1 minute at 100%.
— Continue cooking at 70% for 5 to 7 minutes, giving the dishes a half-turn halfway through the cooking time.
— Remove from the oven and drain off the fat.
— Let stand for 3 minutes before serving.

MICROTIPS

Rapid Blanching of Vegetables
Put 500 mL (2 cups) of vegetables, cut into small pieces (2.5 cm or 1 inch lengths) and 50 mL (1/4 cup) of water in a freezer bag and then

vacuum seal.
–Cook 2 minutes at 100% or until the vegetables are a bright and uniform color.
–Remove from the oven and plunge immediately into ice water to stop the cooking process.
–Label the contents of the bag with the date of freezing as well as the maximum storage time and place in the freezer.

Freezing for Easier Defrosting
When time is at a premium, your freezing methods should facilitate quick defrosting. Using round containers that can go directly into the microwave oven will save time and dishes. When preparing meals for one or two, the defrosting and cooking are greatly simplified when food has been packaged in individual servings.

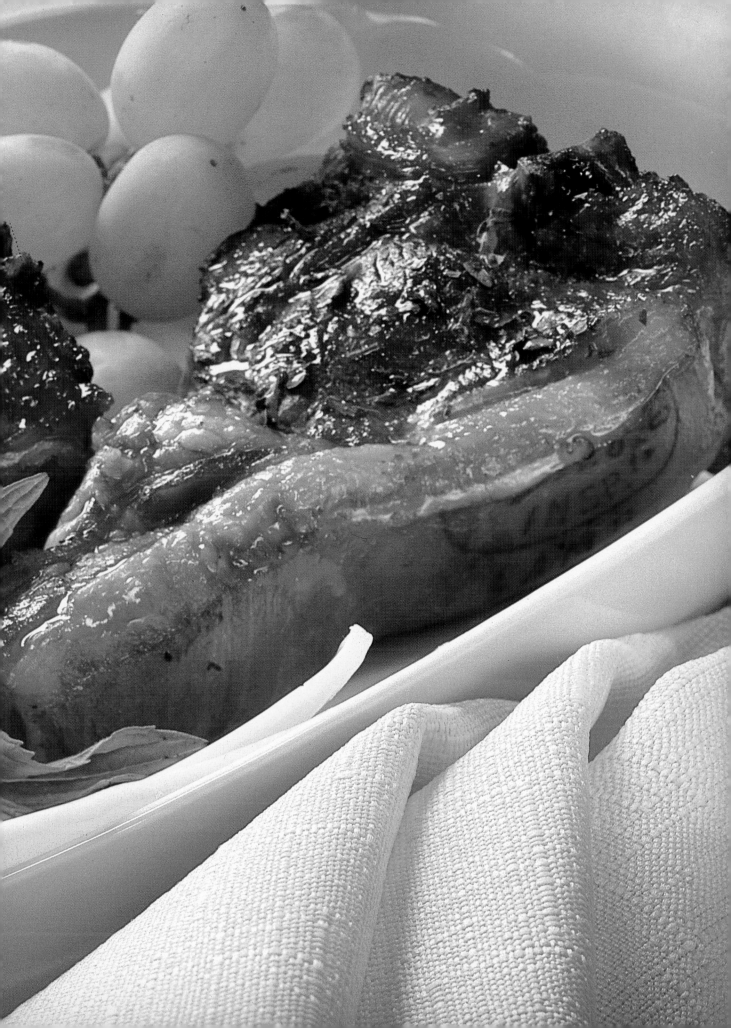

Country Omelette

Level of Difficulty	🍴
Preparation Time	15 min
Cost per Serving	**$**
Number of Servings	2
Nutritional Value	293 calories 17.3 g protein 3.1 mg iron
Food Exchanges	2.5 oz meat 1 vegetable exchange 1/2 bread exchange 1 fat exchange
Cooking Time	9 min
Standing Time	4 min
Power Level	100%
Write Your Cooking Time Here	

Ingredients
3 large eggs
2 slices bacon, cut into pieces
1 onion, coarsely chopped
1 potato, cooked and diced
6 mushrooms, sliced
30 mL (2 tablespoons) milk
pinch fine herbs
salt and pepper to taste
50 mL (1/4 cup) Gruyère cheese, grated
paprika to garnish

Method
— Place the bacon in a dish and cook for 2 minutes at 100%.
— Add the onion and potato; cover and cook at 100% for 2 minutes, stirring once during the cooking.
— Add the mushrooms, cover and continue cooking for 1 minute at 100%.
— Stir and allow to stand for 2 minutes.
— In a bowl, beat the eggs and add the milk and seasonings.
— Add to the vegetable mixture and stir.
— Cook for 1 minute at 100% and stir.
— Continue to cook for 1 to 2 minutes.
— Sprinkle with the Gruyère cheese and garnish with paprika.
— Cook for 1 minute at 100%.
— Let stand for 2 minutes and serve.

Gather these ingredients and in less than half an hour you can produce a flavorful omelette.

Add the mushrooms to the bacon, onion and potato mixture.

Stir the omelette after 1 minute to ensure even cooking.

Rice with Vegetables

Level of Difficulty	
Preparation Time	20 min
Cost per Serving	**$**
Number of Servings	2
Nutritional Value	149 calories 5.5 g protein 33.2 g carbohydrate
Food Exchanges	2 1/2 vegetable exchanges 1 bread exchange
Cooking Time	15 min
Standing Time	5 min
Power Level	100%, 70%
Write Your Cooking Time Here	

Ingredients
125 mL (1/2 cup) long grain rice
2 leeks, white parts only, sliced
1 carrot, diced
1 onion, sliced
250 mL (1 cup) hot chicken broth
2 mL (1/2 teaspoon) cumin
2 mL (1/2 teaspoon) coriander
pinch cayenne
salt and pepper to taste
1/2 apple, peeled and coarsely chopped

Method
— Place the leeks, carrots and onions in a dish and add one quarter of the chicken broth.
— Cover and cook at 100% for 3 to 4 minutes, stirring halfway through the cooking time.
— Add the remaining broth and all the other ingredients except for the apple.
— Cook for 3 minutes at 100%.
— Stir and reduce the power to 70%; continue cooking for 6 to 8 minutes.
— Add the apple and stir.
— Cover and allow to stand for 5 minutes before serving.

Assemble these ingredients and, presto—create an exceptionally flavorful dish.

Cook the leeks, carrots and onions in 50 mL (1/4 cup) of the chicken broth.

MICROTIPS

How To Choose Leeks

Choose leeks that are smooth and glossy, with straight and thick stalks, white roots and green tails.

Leeks will keep about one week in the refrigerator. Wash well before cooking as sand and dirt collect between the tightly packed layers and are difficult to remove.

89

Strawberry Shortcake

Level of Difficulty	
Preparation Time	15 min*
Cost per Serving	$
Number of Servings	2
Nutritional Value	410 calories 6 g protein 25 g carbohydrate
Food Exchanges	1 fruit exchange 1 bread exchange 8 fat exchanges
Cooking Time	2 min
Standing Time	5 min
Power Level	70%
Write Your Cooking Time Here	

* The cakes must be allowed to cool before being assembled for serving.

Ingredients
10 strawberries, sliced
125 mL (1/2 cup) 35%
cream, whipped
90 mL (6 tablespoons) flour
2 mL (1/2 teaspoon) baking
powder
pinch salt
45 mL (3 tablespoons) butter
15 mL (1 tablespoon) sugar
2 egg yolks

Method
— Combine the flour, baking powder and salt, and set aside.
— Cream the butter and sugar, add the egg yolks and mix well. Blend in the flour mixture.
— Grease the bottom and sides of 2 ramekins with a small amount of oil, butter or Pam and place equal amounts of the mixture in each.
— Place the ramekins on a raised rack in the oven and cook for 1 1/2 to 2 minutes at 70%, giving them a half-turn halfway through cooking.
— Let stand for 5 minutes.
— Unmold the cakes from the ramekins and allow them to cool.
— Cut the cakes in half lengthwise and place half the whipped cream and strawberries on the two bottom halves.
— Place the top halves on the filling and garnish with the remaining cream and strawberries.

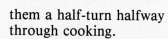

Gather these ingredients for this exquisite dessert, perfect for any occasion.

After greasing the ramekins, place an equal amount of the batter in each.

MICROTIPS

Defrosting Half a Package of Frozen Vegetables

To defrost half a package of frozen vegetables wrap the portion you wish to keep frozen in aluminum foil and defrost the package in the microwave. The remaining vegetables can be put back in the freezer in an airtight container.

Individual Cheesecakes

Level of Difficulty	🍴🍴 🍴🍴
Preparation Time	20 min*
Cost per Serving	**$**
Number of Servings	2
Nutritional Value	255 calories 4.4 g protein 23.2 mg iron
Food Exchanges	1 oz meat 1 fruit exchange 1 bread exchange 1 fat exchange
Cooking Time	2 min 10 sec
Standing Time	none
Power Level	90%, 70%, 100%
Write Your Cooking Time Here	

* **The cheesecakes should be thoroughly chilled in the refrigerator before serving.**

Ingredients

Crust:
5 mL (1 teaspoon) soft butter
15 mL (1 tablespoon) sugar
30 mL (2 tablespoons) flour

Filling:
60 g (2 oz) cream cheese
1 egg yolk
15 mL (1 tablespoon) sugar
15 mL (1 tablespoon) orange juice
2 mL (1/2 teaspoon) orange zest
pinch nutmeg
pinch salt

Glaze:
10 mL (2 teaspoons) apricot jam
5 mL (1 teaspoon) orange juice

Method

— Place large paper cupcake liners in 2 ramekins.
— Mix all the ingredients for the crust and put equal amounts into each ramekin.
— Press the mixture against the bottom and up the sides to form a lining.
— Place the ramekins on a raised rack in the microwave and cook for 30 to 40 seconds at 90%. Set aside.
— To prepare the filling, beat the cream cheese, add the egg yolk and beat again.
— Add the sugar, orange juice and zest, nutmeg and salt, and mix well.
— Put equal amounts of the filling into each crust.
— Place the ramekins on a rack in the oven and cook for 45 to 60 seconds at 70%. Put into the

refrigerator to chill
thoroughly.
— To prepare the glaze, mix
the jam with the orange
juice and cook for 20 to
30 seconds at 100%.
— Spread the glaze over
each cheesecake before
serving.

To save time, gather all the
ingredients required for this
recipe before beginning.

Press the mixture for the crust
against the bottom and up the
sides of the cupcake liners
before cooking.

Chantilly Almond Cream

Level of Difficulty	🍴
Preparation Time	15 min*
Cost per Serving	$ $
Number of Servings	2
Nutritional Value	550 calories 7.6 g protein 47.6 g lipids
Food Exchanges	1 oz meat 8 1/2 fat exchanges
Cooking Time	1 min 30 sec
Standing Time	none
Power Level	100%
Write Your Cooking Time Here	

* The almonds must be cooled in the refrigerator during preparation of the recipe.

Ingredients
75 mL (1/3 cup) almonds
45 mL (3 tablespoons) butter
1 egg white
30 mL (2 tablespoons) sugar
15 mL (1 tablespoon) crème de cacao
125 mL (1/2 cup) 35% cream

Method
— Place the almonds and butter in a dish and cook at 100% for 1 to 1-1/2 minutes or until the almonds are roasted, stirring once during the cooking.
— Allow the almond mixture to cool in the refrigerator.
— Crush half the almond mixture.
— In a bowl, beat the egg white until stiff; slowly add half the sugar.
— add half the sugar.
— Whip the cream, adding the remaining sugar.
— Add the crème de cacao and crushed almonds to the whipped cream and then add to the beaten egg white.
— Pour this mixture into serving dishes and garnish with the remaining almonds before serving.

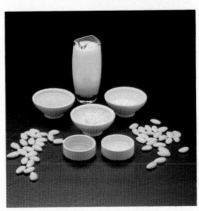

Before beginning this delicious recipe, gather all the necessary ingredients.

In a bowl, whip the cream and add the remaining sugar.

Add the crème de cacao and crushed almonds to the whipped cream and then add to the beaten egg white.

Entertaining

To distract the hearts of lovers or to tempt the palate of the solitary diner, we have devised a menu outstanding for its flavor and freshness.

The hors d'œuvre of peach halves stuffed with shrimp mousse will tempt even the most sophisticated appetite. Trout with capers provides a delicious main course, well seasoned but with a subtle flavor, complemented by the salad, an unusual combination of mushrooms and cauliflower. Such are the delicious treats that await you along with the finishing touch: a delightful dessert of pineapple and strawberries.

From the Recipe to Your Table

Even when you're cooking for only one or two, a meal that is not properly planned can become a disaster. Whether you are preparing a meal using a microwave oven or a conventional oven, the planning stage is the same. Only the cooking and reheating times are different.

The morning before the meal:
—Prepare the mushroom and cauliflower salad without adding the dressing.
—Prepare the shrimp mousse.

2 hours before the meal:
—Prepare the pineapple dessert.

1 hour before the meal:
—Add the dressing to the salad.

45 minutes before the meal:
—Place the trout in the marinade.

15 minutes before the meal:
—Cook the trout.

10 minutes before the meal:
—Prepare the peach halves.

Peach Halves with Shrimp Mousse

Ingredients
1 peach
115 g (4 oz) shrimp, cooked and chopped
50 mL (1/4 cup) celery, finely chopped
15 mL (1 tablespoon) fresh parsley, chopped
15 mL (1 tablespoon) 35% cream
15 mL (1 tablespoon) butter, melted
10 mL (2 teaspoons) cognac
lettuce leaves

Method
— In a blender, mix the shrimp, celery and parsley to a smooth consistency.
— Add the cream, butter and cognac.
— Blend until puréed.
— Cover and refrigerate for at least 1 hour.
— Peel the peach, cut in half and remove the pit.
— Stuff the peach halves with the shrimp mousse and serve on a bed of lettuce.

Mushroom and Cauliflower Salad

Ingredients
1/2 cauliflower
10 large mushrooms
1/2 lemon
30 mL (2 tablespoons)
Parmesan cheese, grated
Vinaigrette:
5 mL (1 teaspoon) Dijon
mustard
15 mL (1 tablespoon) fresh
parsley, chopped
45 mL (3 tablespoons) wine
vinegar
125 mL (1/2 cup) oil
salt and pepper to taste

Method
— Cut the cauliflower into
  flowerets and wash.
— Place the flowerets in a
  dish, cover and cook for
  3 to 4 minutes at 100%.
— Drain the cauliflower and
  allow it to cool.
— Slice the mushrooms and
  toss in a salad bowl with
  the cauliflower.
— Squeeze the lemon over
  the vegetables and set
  them aside.

— Prepare the vinaigrette by
  mixing the mustard,
  parsley and wine vinegar;
  stirring constantly, add
  the oil in a fine stream.
  Season to taste.
— Pour the vinaigrette over
  the vegetables 1 hour
  before serving and
  sprinkle with Parmesan
  just before serving.

Trout with Capers

Level of Difficulty	¶¶¶
Preparation Time	10 min*
Cost per Serving	$ $
Number of Servings	2
Nutritional Value	759 calories 40.9 g protein 67.7 mg lipids
Food Exchanges	7 oz meat 5 fat exchanges
Cooking Time	7 min
Standing Time	3 min
Power Level	100%, 70%
Write Your Cooking Time Here	

* The trout should marinate for 30 minutes at room temperature before cooking.

Ingredients
2 trout, trimmed and cleaned
30 mL (2 tablespoons) lemon juice
30 mL (2 tablespoons) oil
1 mL (1/4 teaspoon) marjoram
2 mL (1/2 teaspoon) lemon zest, grated
50 mL (1/4 cup) oil
30 mL (2 tablespoons) capers

Method
— In a bowl, mix the lemon juice, 30 mL (2 tablespoons) oil, marjoram and lemon zest to make the marinade.
— Place the trout in the marinade, spooning the marinade over them.
— Allow to marinate for 30 minutes at room temperature, turning them over several times during this period.
— Remove the trout and dry; set the marinade aside.
— Preheat a browning dish for 7 minutes at 100%, add 50 mL (1/4 cup) oil and heat 30 seconds at 100%.
— Sear the trout on each side and add the marinade.
— Cover, reduce the power to 70%.
— Cook for 5 to 7 minutes, giving the dish a half-turn midway through the cooking time.
— Garnish with capers and let stand for 3 minutes before serving.

Fruit-Filled Pineapple

Ingredients
1 small pineapple
125 mL (1/2 cup)
strawberries
60 mL (4 tablespoons) sugar
30 mL (2 tablespoons) kirsch
50 mL (1/4 cup) 35% cream,
whipped

Method
— With a sharp knife, cut
   the pineapple in half.
— Cut out the pulp and set
   the pineapple shells aside;
   cut the pineapple pulp
   into small cubes.
— Mix the pineapple cubes
   with the strawberries;
   divide this mixture
   equally into the pineapple
   shells.
— Sprinkle with sugar and
   then with kirsch.
— Garnish with whipped
   cream just before serving.

Cooking Vegetables

Why deny yourself a favorite
vegetable when it can be
cooked to perfection in your
microwave oven? The chart
on the right will give you
some useful information on
recommended water
quantities and cooking times.
For more detailed
instructions, consult
Vegetables, Volume 13, in
this series.

Vegetable (Fresh)	Quantity	Water Quantity	Cooking time at 100% (in minutes)
Asparagus	225 g (8 oz)	50 mL (1/4 cup)	2 to 3
Beans,	225 g (8 oz)	50 mL (1/4 cup)	6 to 9
Beets, sliced	225 g (8 oz)	75 mL (1/3 cup)	7 to 9
Broccoli (flowerets)	1/2 bunch	30 mL (2 tbsp)	3 to 4
Brussels sprouts	225 g (8 oz)	30 mL (2 tbsp)	3 to 5
Carrots, sliced	225 g (8 oz)	50 mL (1/4 cup)	5 to 7
Cauliflower (flowerets)	1 small	30 mL (2 tbsp)	4 to 5
Celery, sliced	125 mL (1/2 cup)	15 mL (1 tbsp)	4 to 5
Corn, on the cob	1 ear 2 ears	none none	3 to 4 5 to 6
Endive	4	30 mL (2 tbsp)	3 to 5
Green cabbage, grated	250 mL (1 cup)	30 mL (2 tbsp)	3 to 5
Leeks, sliced	4	30 mL (2 tbsp)	3 to 5
Mushrooms, sliced	225 g (8 oz)	none	2 to 3
Parsnips, cut into cubes	225 g (8 oz)	50 mL (1/4 cup)	5 to 7
Peppers, sliced	2	30 mL (2 tbsp)	3 to 5
Potatoes, whole	1 2	none none	2 to 3 3 to 4
Rutabaga, cut into cubes	225 g (8 oz)	50 mL (1/4 cup)	5 to 7
Spinach	225 g (8 oz)	none	2 to 3
Zucchini, sliced	225 g (8 oz)	30 mL (2 tbsp)	3 to 5

Wine Terminology

Have you ever wanted to describe a wine you especially enjoyed and found yourself at a loss for words? We've prepared a short list of terms most often used to describe wines that may help you.

Acidic: A description of a wine that is very dry but somewhat sharp.

Aroma: The characteristic odor of an individual wine, dependent on the variety of grape used.

Bouquet: The aroma of a wine after it has lost its grapey fragrance.

Breed: A term used to describe wines that are distinguished and of superior quality.

Brut: Champagne of the driest type.

Character: The very definite qualities by which a wine can easily be recognized.

Corked or corky: This defect refers to a wine that has been spoiled by a cork infected with mold.

Delicate: Describes a wine of low alcoholic content with a light and subtle flavor; a delicate wine cannot lay claim to being a great wine.

Dry: Indicates a lack of sugar; applies mainly to white wines.

Fruity: Describes the fragrance or flavor of certain young wines.

Green: This term refers to wines that taste of unripe grapes: they are too acid, raw and harsh, thus lacking softness and maturity.

Harvest: The gathering of ripened grapes to be used for wine making.

Hearty: Full-bodied, straightforward, high-alcohol red wine.

Lively: Describes the character of a fresh, fruity young wine with the appropriate degree of acidity.

Nouveau: A red wine that is less than a year old.

Robe: Refers to the general color of a wine.

The production and sale of wines has grown into such an important industry that it has become imperative to have government controls in order to protect the consumer as well as the producer. With this in mind, very strong legislation has been enacted in France. The French legislation recognizes three categories of wine: *Appellation d'Origine Controlée, Vins Délimité de Qualité Supérieur* and Table Wine.

Vinosity: The essential quality or character of a wine, achieved by accentuating the best characteristics of the particular type.

Appellation d'Origine Controlée: Literally, the controlled place of origin, this designation is applied to wines that meet very high standards in terms of the following criteria:
1. place of origin;
2. variety of grape used;
3. minimum alcohol content;
4. soil composition;
5. maximum limitations on yield per acre;
6. wine-making practices, i.e., aging process, quality control, etc.

Vins Délimités de Qualité Supérieure: In this category, we find wines that are good enough to be subject to quality control but do not quite fit into the top category. French legislation controls the following:
1. variety of grape used;
2. minimum alcohol content;
3. area of production.

Table Wine: This designation applies to ordinary wines on sale at liquor stores. The labels must indicate content and percentage of alcohol.

MICROTIPS

Wines to Accompany Your Meals

Wine is always a welcome addition to a meal whether you have company or are eating alone. Here is a short list of wines and the food they complement especially well.

Dry white wine: eggs, hors d'oeuvres, fish, poultry, seafood, veal, cheeses.

Sweet and fruity white wine: fish and spicy seafood, fruit dishes, dishes with creamed sauces.

Dry Champagne can be served with every course during a meal.

Full-bodied red wines: red meat and strong cheeses, dishes with tomato sauce.

Lighter red wines: white meat, poultry, lamb, pork, sausage and cheeses.

Utensils and Dishes for the Microwave Oven

If you have just obtained a microwave oven, do not rush out to buy a complete set of special utensils and dishes. Most dishes and containers made of plastic and glass can be used. However, if you do wish to purchase dishes especially designed for microwave ovens, here is a list of the most useful items along with a brief description of each.

All-purpose measure: A glass or pyrex measuring container that resembles a measuring cup but is larger. It is useful for mixing ingredients as well as for cooking them.

Bacon rack: Because the grooves keep food from coming into contact with the cooking juices, the bacon rack has uses other than cooking bacon; it can be used for cooking fish, poultry and meat as well as for defrosting.

Browning dish: This dish has a special coating, usually ferrite, on the bottom. The ferrite absorbs the microwaves and the dish gets very hot. This enables you to sear or brown meats and to sauté vegetables for a stir-fry.

Covered casserole: Many recipes call for cooking in covered dishes. Using a cover prevents moisture from escaping and, thus, the food from drying out.

Rack: A plastic roasting rack which is grooved and can be placed in a larger dish so that meat does not come into contact with its juices while cooking. Similar to a bacon rack.

Ramekins: Small round individual baking dishes; frequently used to serve pâtés, individual meat loaves, mousses and soufflés.

Tube pan or ring dish: A dish with a round shape and a raised tube in the center that helps to ensure even cooking of food. It can also be used to mold foods to be frozen.

Conversion Chart

**Conversion Chart for the
Main Measures Used in
Cooking**

Volume

1 teaspoon............ 5 mL
1 tablespoon........ 15 mL

1 quart (4 cups)....... 1 litre
1 pint (2 cups)...... 500 mL
1/2 cup............ 125 mL
1/4 cup............ 50 mL

Weight

2.2 lb......... 1 kg (1000 g)
1.1 lb............... 500 g
0.5 lb............... 225 g
0.25 lb.............. 115 g

1 oz................ 30 g

**Metric Equivalents
for Cooking
Temperatures**

49°C...............	120°F	120°C...............	250°F
54°C...............	130°F	135°C...............	275°F
60°C...............	140°F	150°C...............	300°F
66°C...............	150°F	160°C...............	325°F
71°C...............	160°F	180°C...............	350°F
77°C...............	170°F	190°C...............	375°F
82°C...............	180°F	200°C...............	400°F
93°C...............	200°F	220°C...............	425°F
107°C...............	225°F	230°C...............	450°F

Readers will note that, in the recipes, we give 250 mL as the equivalent for 1 cup and 450 g as the equivalent for 1 lb and that fractions of these measurements are even less mathematically accurate. The reason for this is that mathematically accurate conversions are just not practical in cooking. Your kitchen scales are simply not accurate enough to weigh 454 g—the true equivalent of 1 lb—and it would be a waste of time to try. The conversions given in this series, therefore, necessarily represent approximate equivalents, but they will still give excellent results in the kitchen. No problems should be encountered if you adhere to either metric or imperial measurements throughout a recipe.

Index

MICROTIPS